MUFFINS

MUFFINS

40 TANTALIZING RECIPES FOR TASTY MUFFINS

This is a Parragon Publishing Book
This edition published in 2006

Parragon Publishing
Queen Street House
4 Queen Street
Bath BA1 1HE, UK

ISBN: 1-40547-418-1

Printed in China

Design concept by Fiona Roberts
Produced by the Bridgewater Book Company Ltd
Photographer: Laurie Evans
Home Economist: Annie Rigg

Notes for the Reader
This book uses imperial, metric, or US cup measurements. Follow the same units of
measurement throughout; do not mix imperial and metric. All spoon measurements are
level; teaspoons are assumed to be 5 ml, and tablespoons are assumed to be 15 ml.
Unless otherwise stated, milk is assumed to be whole, eggs and individual vegetables
such as potatoes are medium, and pepper is freshly ground black pepper. Recipes using
raw or very lightly cooked eggs should be avoided by infants, the elderly, pregnant women,
convalescents, and anyone suffering from an illness.

Picture acknowledgment
The Bridgewater Book Company would like to thank Simon Jauncey/Stone/Getty Images for
permission to reproduce copyright material for the endpapers.

contents

There's something so satisfying about baking a batch of muffins. Perhaps it's because they're so quick and easy to make, because there are so many delicious variations, from fresh fruit to chocolate, or simply because they look and smell so wonderfully appetizing. Even so, the pleasure of making them is secondary to the bliss of biting into the warm, melt-in-the-mouth texture of a freshly baked muffin.

Everyone loves muffins, but you'd probably never get them to agree on which type is the best, with some voting for spicy apple muffins, others for savory cheese, and probably quite a lot for chocolate. So it's just as well that this book contains a comprehensive collection of perennially popular recipes. In addition, it also offers some clever new ideas for both sweet and savory treats.

The recipes are divided into four chapters, making it easy to find just the right one. Sweet Indulgences are everyday family bakes, often made with pantry ingredients. Healthy Choices provides some smart ideas for those trying to reduce their intake of fat and sugar but who still have a sweet tooth. Savory Muffins is full of delicious and unusual lunchtime snacks and perfect picnic suggestions, while the recipes in Special Occasions provide both the means and excuse for a party.

There's nothing like a warm muffin with a cup of coffee during a well-earned midmorning break or as a tasty snack for ravenous children when they come home from school. This chapter is packed with family favorites—and perhaps a few surprises—for just such occasions. However, beware—if news of your baking prowess gets round, you may find a whole class of children dropping in on their way home.

Fresh and dried fruit, warm spices, chopped nuts, and, of course, chocolate are among the featured flavors. There are recipes for popular, classic combinations, such as Apple and Cinnamon Muffins and Chocolate Orange Muffins, as well as for some more unusual mixtures that you might like to try, such as Nectarine and Banana Muffins and Lime and Poppy Seed Muffins.

SWEET INDULGENCES

All these recipes are very quick and easy, yet taste fabulous. It's simplicity itself to rustle up a batch for breakfast or when unexpected guests arrive. They cook in no time at all and you don't have to wait for them to cool because there are no extra toppings to spread. In any case, they smell so appetizing and taste so delicious when freshly baked that it would be virtually impossible to prevent the family from instantly indulging themselves.

If by any strange chance these muffins are not all scoffed instantly, you can store them in an airtight container. They will keep for a day or two, but are always much better eaten on the day they are baked, whether warm or cold.

MAKES 12

3 tbsp soft margarine

1 cup superfine sugar

2 large eggs

2/3 cup whole plain yogurt

5 tbsp milk

2 cups all-purpose flour

1 tsp baking soda

1 cup semisweet chocolate chips

Chocolate Chip Muffins

The batter can also be used to make 6 large or 24 mini muffins. Bake mini muffins for 10 minutes, or until springy to the touch.

• Preheat the oven to 400°F/200°C. Line a 12-cup muffin pan with muffin paper liners.
• Place the margarine and sugar in a mixing bowl and beat with a wooden spoon until light and fluffy. Beat in the eggs, yogurt, and milk until combined.
• Sift the flour and baking soda into the batter. Stir until just blended.
• Stir in the chocolate chips, then divide the batter evenly between the paper liners and bake in the oven for 25 minutes, or until risen and golden. Remove the muffins from the oven and let cool in the pan for 5 minutes, then place them on a cooling rack to cool completely.

MAKES 6

scant 2/3 cup all-purpose whole
 wheat flour
1/2 cup all-purpose white flour
1 1/2 tsp baking powder
pinch of salt
1 tsp ground cinnamon

scant 1/4 cup golden superfine sugar
2 small eating apples, peeled, cored,
 and finely chopped
1/2 cup milk
1 egg, beaten
4 tbsp butter, melted

TOPPING

12 brown sugar lumps, coarsely
 crushed
1/2 tsp ground cinnamon

Apple and Cinnamon Muffins

These spicy muffins are quick and easy to make with just a few stock ingredients and two small apples. The crunchy sugar topping is a treat.

• Preheat the oven to 400°F/200°C. Place 6 muffin paper liners in a muffin pan.

• Sift both flours, baking powder, salt, and cinnamon together into a large bowl and stir in the sugar and chopped apples. Place the milk, egg, and butter in a separate bowl and mix. Add the wet ingredients to the dry ingredients and gently stir until just combined.

• Divide the batter evenly between the paper liners. To make the topping, mix the crushed sugar lumps and cinnamon together and sprinkle over the muffins. Bake in the oven for 20–25 minutes, or until risen and golden. Remove the muffins from the oven and serve warm or place them on a cooling rack and let cool.

MAKES 12

scant 1½ cups all-purpose flour

⅓ cup unsweetened cocoa, plus
   extra for dusting

1 tbsp baking powder

1 tsp ground cinnamon

generous ½ cup golden superfine
   sugar

6½ oz/185 g white chocolate, broken
   into pieces

2 large eggs

generous ⅓ cup sunflower-seed or
   peanut oil

1 cup milk

Double Chocolate Muffins

*When stirring the muffin
batter together, do not
overstir or the muffins will
be tough. The batter should
be quite lumpy.*

• Preheat the oven to 400°F/200°C. Line a 12-cup muffin pan with muffin paper liners. Sift the flour, cocoa, baking powder, and cinnamon into a large mixing bowl. Stir in the sugar and 4½ oz/125 g of the white chocolate.
• Place the eggs and oil in a separate bowl and whisk until frothy, then gradually whisk in the milk. Stir into the dry ingredients until just blended. Divide the batter evenly between the paper liners, filling each three-quarters full. Bake in the oven for 20 minutes, or until well risen and springy to the touch. Remove the muffins from the oven, let cool in the pan for 2 minutes, then remove them and place them on a cooling rack to cool completely.
• Place the remaining white chocolate in a heatproof bowl, set the bowl over a pan of barely simmering water, and heat until melted. Spread over the top of the muffins. Let set, then dust the tops with a little cocoa and serve.

MAKES 8

generous 1 cup all-purpose flour

1½ tsp baking powder

pinch of salt

⅓ cup golden superfine sugar

1 cup shelled pecans, coarsely
  chopped

2 large ripe bananas, mashed

5 tbsp milk

2 tbsp butter, melted

1 large egg, beaten

½ tsp vanilla extract

Banana Pecan Muffins

This is a good way of
using up ripe bananas.
Try hazelnuts or walnuts
instead of pecans.

• Preheat the oven to 375°F/190°C. Place 8 muffin paper liners in a muffin pan. Sift the flour, baking powder and salt into a bowl, add the sugar and pecans, and stir to combine.

• Place the mashed bananas, milk, butter, egg, and vanilla extract in a separate bowl and mix together. Add the wet ingredients to the dry ingredients and gently stir until just combined.

• Divide the batter evenly between the paper liners and bake in the oven for 20–25 minutes until risen and golden. Remove the muffins from the oven and place them on a cooling rack and let cool.

MAKES 12

generous 1¾ cups all-purpose flour

4 tsp baking powder

generous ⅜ cup superfine sugar

6 tbsp crunchy peanut butter

1 large egg, beaten

4 tbsp butter, melted

¾ cup milk

5½ oz/150 g vanilla fudge, cut into
small pieces

3 tbsp coarsely chopped unsalted
peanuts

Fudge Nut Muffins

The chewy pieces of fudge used in these muffins give them a lovely texture and provide a nice contrast to the crunchiness of the nuts. Store the muffins in airtight containers.

• Preheat the oven to 400°F/200°C. Line a 12-cup muffin pan with double muffin paper liners. Sift the flour and baking powder into a bowl. Stir in the superfine sugar. Add the peanut butter and stir until the mixture resembles bread crumbs.

• Place the egg, butter, and milk in a separate bowl and beat until blended, then stir into the dry ingredients until just blended. Lightly stir in the fudge pieces. Divide the batter evenly between the muffin liners.

• Sprinkle the chopped peanuts on top and bake in the oven for 20–25 minutes until well risen and firm to the touch. Remove the muffins from the oven and let cool for 2 minutes, then place them on a cooling rack to cool completely.

MAKES 8–10

sunflower-seed or peanut oil,
    for oiling
scant 1 cup self-rising white flour
scant 1 cup self-rising whole wheat
    flour
generous ¼ cup ground almonds

generous ¼ cup packed brown sugar
rind and juice of 1 orange
¾ cup cream cheese
2 large eggs
⅓ cup semisweet chocolate chips

Chocolate Orange Muffins

These muffins are a favorite with children of all ages. They are best served warm and are particularly good for breakfast.

• Preheat the oven to 375°F/190°C. Thoroughly oil 10 cups of a 12-cup muffin pan.
• Sift both flours into a mixing bowl and stir in the ground almonds and sugar.
• Mix the orange rind and juice, cream cheese, and eggs together in a separate bowl. Make a well in the center of the dry ingredients and stir in the wet ingredients, then add the chocolate chips. Beat well to combine all the ingredients.
• Divide the batter evenly between the cups, filling each no more than three-quarters full.
• Bake in the oven for 20–25 minutes until well risen and golden brown.
• Remove from the oven and let cool slightly on a cooling rack, but eat them as fresh as possible.

MAKES 12

generous ⅓ cup sunflower-seed
   or peanut oil, plus extra for oiling
   (if using)
generous 1¾ cups all-purpose flour
1 tsp baking soda
¼ tsp salt
¼ tsp allspice
½ cup superfine sugar

½ cup shelled almonds, chopped
6 oz/175 g ripe nectarine, peeled
   and chopped
1 ripe banana, sliced
2 large eggs
⅓ cup thick strained plain or
   banana-flavored yogurt
1 tsp almond extract

Nectarine and Banana Muffins

To add a delicious crunchy topping to these muffins, put 3 tablespoons raw sugar and 1 teaspoon allspice in a small bowl and mix together well. Just before transferring the muffins to the oven, sprinkle some of the spiced sugar over each muffin.

• Preheat the oven to 400°F/200°C. Oil a 12-cup muffin pan with sunflower-seed oil, or line it with 12 muffin paper liners. Sift the flour, baking soda, salt, and allspice into a mixing bowl. Then add the superfine sugar and chopped almonds and stir together.

• In a separate large bowl, mash the nectarine and banana together, then stir in the eggs, remaining sunflower-seed oil, yogurt, and almond extract. Add the mashed fruit mixture to the flour mixture and then gently stir together until just combined. Do not overstir the batter—it is fine for it to be a little lumpy.

• Divide the muffin batter evenly between the 12 cups in the muffin pan or the paper liners (they should be about two-thirds full). Transfer to the oven and bake for 20 minutes, or until risen and golden. Remove the muffins from the oven and serve warm, or place them on a cooling rack and let cool.

MAKES 12

¾ cup sunflower-seed or peanut oil,
    plus extra for oiling (if using)

1½ cups all-purpose flour

1 tsp baking powder

½ tsp salt

generous 1⅛ cups superfine sugar

1 large egg

1 large egg white

⅔ cup milk

1 tbsp lime juice

1 tbsp grated lime rind

2 tsp poppy seeds

TO DECORATE

2 tsp grated lime rind

1–2 tsp poppy seeds

Lime and Poppy Seed Muffins

To ring the changes, why not try varying the flavor? You can substitute the same quantity of lemon juice and rind for the lime, or for a milder flavor, use the same quantity of orange juice and rind instead of the lime.

- Preheat the oven to 375°F/190°C. Oil a 12-cup muffin pan with sunflower-seed oil, or line it with 12 muffin paper liners. Sift the flour, baking powder, and salt into a mixing bowl. Then add the superfine sugar and stir together.
- In a separate bowl, whisk the egg, egg white, remaining sunflower-seed oil, and milk together, then stir in the lime juice and grated lime rind. Add the egg mixture to the flour mixture, then add the poppy seeds and gently stir together. Do not overstir the batter—it is fine for it to be a little lumpy.
- Divide the muffin batter evenly between the 12 cups in the muffin pan or the paper liners (they should be about two-thirds full). Sprinkle over grated lime rind and poppy seeds to decorate, then bake in the oven for 25 minutes, or until risen and golden. Remove the muffins from the oven and serve warm, or place them on a cooling rack and let cool.

MAKES 12

2 tbsp sunflower-seed or peanut oil,
  plus extra for oiling (if using)

generous 1¾ cups all-purpose flour

1 tsp baking soda

½ tsp salt

1 cup raw sugar

⅝ cup dried figs, chopped

1 cup almonds, chopped

1 cup water

1 tsp almond extract

2 tbsp chopped almonds, to decorate

Fig and Almond Muffins

You can replace the dried figs with the same quantity of no-soak dried dates or apricots. And why not try replacing the almonds with the same quantity of walnuts or pecans? Try your own combinations to vary the flavor.

• Preheat the oven to 375°F/190°C. Oil a 12-cup muffin pan with sunflower-seed oil, or line it with 12 muffin paper liners. Sift the flour, baking soda, and salt into a mixing bowl. Then add the raw sugar and stir together.

• In a separate bowl, mix the figs, almonds, and remaining sunflower-seed oil together. Then stir in the water and almond extract. Add the fruit and nut mixture to the flour mixture and gently stir together. Do not overstir—it is fine for it to be a little lumpy.

• Divide the muffin batter evenly between the 12 cups in the muffin pan or the paper liners (they should be about two-thirds full), then sprinkle over the remaining chopped almonds to decorate. Transfer to the oven and bake for 25 minutes, or until risen and golden. Remove the muffins from the oven and serve warm, or place them on a cooling rack and let cool.

MAKES 12

3½ oz/100 g butter, softened

generous ⅝ cup superfine sugar

½ cup packed brown sugar

2 large eggs

⅔ cup sour cream

5 tbsp milk

generous 1¾ cups all-purpose flour

1 tsp baking soda

2 tbsp unsweetened cocoa

1 tsp allspice

generous 1 cup semisweet
  chocolate chips

Spiced Chocolate Muffins

You can replace the allspice
with ground cinnamon or
with a mixture of equal
parts nutmeg and cloves.

• Preheat the oven to 375°F/190°C. Line a 12-cup muffin pan with muffin paper liners.

• Place the butter, superfine sugar, and brown sugar in a bowl and beat well. Beat in the eggs, sour cream, and milk until thoroughly mixed. Sift the flour, baking soda, cocoa, and allspice into a separate bowl and stir into the mixture. Add the chocolate chips and mix well. Divide the batter evenly between the paper liners. Bake in the oven for 25–30 minutes.

• Remove from the oven and let cool for 10 minutes. Place them on a cooling rack and let cool completely. Store in an airtight container until required.

There's no reason why just because you're counting the calories or trying to follow a healthy diet you should miss out on the pleasures of home-baked treats. The judicious use of lowfat ingredients and the imaginative substitution of the natural sweetness of fruit for added refined sugar are just two of the ways suggested for making healthy choices.

The recipes in this chapter are the proof that being careful about using healthier ingredients doesn't in any way sacrifice flavor or variety. Indeed, you could serve any of this fabulous batch of muffins to family and friends and they wouldn't even be able to tell the difference. There's even a recipe for Sugarless Chocolate Muffins, so you can spoil yourself without spoiling your good dietary intentions.

HEALTHY CHOICES

While reducing levels of fats and sugars in their diet is among the main concerns of people aiming for a healthier lifestyle, recipes in this chapter also address other considerations. Intolerance to dairy products is on the increase and such ingredients are also thought to aggravate other conditions, such as some types of eczema. Once again, you don't have to miss out as there are muffins that are completely dairy-free and utterly scrumptious.

Of course, eating well is not just a case of going without things. Try the High-Energy Muffins for breakfast and put a real spring in your step. Nutritionists regard this as the most important meal of the day, but we often fail to eat enough for it to be of real benefit, or even skip it entirely. Starting off the day with an energy-enhancing boost is not only sensible but also a pleasure.

MAKES 10

2 cups self-rising whole wheat flour

2 tsp baking powder

2 tbsp brown sugar

generous ½ cup no-soak dried
  apricots, finely chopped

1 banana, mashed with 1 tbsp
  orange juice

1 tsp finely grated orange rind

1¼ cups skim milk

1 large egg, beaten

3 tbsp sunflower-seed or peanut oil

2 tbsp rolled oats

fruit spread, honey, or maple syrup, to
  serve

Fruity Muffins

If you like dried figs, they make a deliciously crunchy alternative to the apricots; they also go very well with the flavor of orange. Other no-soak dried fruit, finely chopped, can be used as well.

• Preheat the oven to 400°F/200°C. Line 10 cups of a 12-cup muffin pan with muffin paper liners. Sift the flour and baking powder into a mixing bowl, adding any husks that remain in the strainer. Stir in the sugar and chopped apricots.

• Make a well in the center and add the mashed banana, orange rind, milk, beaten egg, and oil. Mix together well to form a thick batter and divide evenly between the muffin liners.

• Sprinkle with a few rolled oats and bake in the oven for 25–30 minutes until well risen and firm to the touch, or until a toothpick inserted into the center comes out clean.

• Remove the muffins from the oven and place them on a cooling rack to cool slightly. Serve the muffins while still warm with a little fruit spread, honey, or maple syrup.

MAKES 18

butter, for greasing

generous 1½ cups all-purpose flour

2 tsp baking powder

½ tsp salt

¼ cup superfine sugar

4 tbsp butter, melted

2 large eggs, lightly beaten

¾ cup milk

1⅛ cups fresh cranberries

¼ cup freshly grated Parmesan
   cheese

Cranberry Muffins

For a sweeter alternative,
replace the Parmesan
cheese with raw sugar.

• Preheat the oven to 400°F/200°C. Lightly grease 2 x 9-cup muffin pans with butter.

• Sift the flour, baking powder, and salt into a mixing bowl. Stir in the superfine sugar.

• In a separate bowl, combine the butter, beaten eggs, and milk, then pour into the bowl of dry ingredients. Mix lightly together until all of the ingredients are evenly combined, then stir in the fresh cranberries.

• Divide the batter evenly between the prepared 18 cups in the muffin pans. Sprinkle the grated Parmesan cheese over the top.

• Transfer to the oven and bake for 20 minutes, or until the muffins are well risen and a golden brown color.

• Remove the muffins from the oven and let them cool slightly in the pans. Place the muffins on a cooling rack and let them cool completely.

MAKES 12

butter, for greasing and serving
   (optional)
6 oz/175 g mealy potatoes, diced
scant 1 cup self-rising flour, plus
   extra for dusting

2 tbsp brown sugar
1 tsp baking powder
scant 1 cup raisins
4 large eggs, separated

Potato and Raisin Muffins

Instead of spreading the
muffins with plain butter,
serve them with cinnamon
butter made by blending
5 tablespoons butter
with a large pinch of
ground cinnamon.

• Preheat the oven to 400°F/200°C. Lightly grease and flour a 12-cup muffin pan. Cook the diced potatoes in a pan of boiling water for 10 minutes, or until tender. Drain well and mash until smooth.
• Transfer the mashed potatoes to a mixing bowl and add the flour, sugar, baking powder, raisins, and egg yolks. Stir well to mix thoroughly.
• In a clean, greasefree bowl, whisk the egg whites until they are standing in peaks. Using a metal spoon, gently fold them into the potato mixture until fully incorporated.
• Divide the batter evenly between the 12 cups in the muffin pan. Bake the muffins in the oven for 10 minutes. Reduce the oven temperature to 325°F/160°C and bake the muffins for an additional 7–10 minutes, or until risen.
• Remove the muffins from the oven and serve warm, buttered, if you like.

MAKES 12

1 large baking apple, peeled, cored,
and thinly sliced

3 tbsp water

1 tsp allspice

2 tbsp sunflower-seed or peanut oil,
plus extra for oiling (if using)

1½ cups all-purpose white or whole
wheat flour

1 tbsp baking powder

¼ tsp salt

⅜ cup wheat germ

⅛ cup fresh raspberries

⅜ cup fresh strawberries,
hulled and chopped

6 tbsp maple syrup

¾ cup apple juice

Dairy-Free Berry Muffins

To make a richer muffin, you can replace the apple juice with the same quantity of soy milk. You can also vary the spices: try using cinnamon or nutmeg instead of the allspice.

• Place the sliced baking apple and water in a pan and bring to a boil. Reduce the heat and stir in half of the allspice, then cover the pan and let simmer, stirring occasionally, for 15–20 minutes until the water has been absorbed. Remove the pan from the heat and let cool. Transfer the apple mixture to a food processor and blend until smooth.

• Preheat the oven to 375°F/190°C. Lightly oil a 12-cup muffin pan with a little sunflower-seed oil, or line it with 12 muffin paper liners.

• Sift the flour, baking powder, salt, and remaining allspice into a mixing bowl. Then stir in the wheat germ.

• In a separate bowl, mix the raspberries, chopped strawberries, maple syrup, remaining oil, puréed apple, and the apple juice together. Add the fruit mixture to the flour mixture and then gently stir together until just combined. Do not overstir the batter—it is fine for it to be a little lumpy.

• Divide the muffin batter evenly between the 12 cups in the muffin pan or the paper liners (they should be about two-thirds full). Transfer to the oven and bake for 25 minutes, or until risen and golden. Remove the muffins from the oven and serve warm, or place them on a cooling rack and let cool.

MAKES 12

5 tbsp sunflower-seed or peanut oil,
    plus extra for oiling (if using)
scant ⅝ cup whole wheat flour
½ cup quick-cooking oats
⅜ cup wheat germ
2 tsp baking powder
1 tsp ground cinnamon
¼ tsp salt

⅓ cup no-soak dried dates,
    pitted and chopped
⅓ cup golden raisins
3½ cups bran flakes
scant 1 cup milk
2 large eggs, beaten
5 tbsp honey
4 tbsp corn syrup
4 tbsp molasses

High-Energy Muffins

These muffins are packed with fast-acting and slow-release carbohydrates, and are therefore great for people who need lots of energy, such as athletes. You can vary the fruit to your taste. For example, try using the same quantity of dried chopped apricots instead of the dates. You can also add a small, ripe, mashed banana to the fruit for extra energy and flavor.

• Preheat the oven to 375°F/190°C. Oil a 12-cup muffin pan with sunflower-seed oil, or line it with 12 muffin paper liners. Place the flour, oats, wheat germ, baking powder, cinnamon, and salt in a mixing bowl and mix together.
• In a separate bowl, mix the dates, golden raisins, and bran flakes together. Pour in the milk and stir together. Then stir in the beaten eggs, honey, corn syrup, molasses, and remaining oil. Add the fruit mixture to the flour mixture and then gently stir together until just combined. Do not overstir the batter—it is fine for it to be a little lumpy.
• Divide the muffin batter evenly between the 12 cups in the muffin pan or the paper liners (they should be about two-thirds full). Transfer to the oven and bake for 20–25 minutes until risen and golden. Remove the muffins from the oven and serve warm, or place them on a cooling rack and let cool.

MAKES 12

4 tbsp sunflower-seed or peanut oil,
   plus extra for oiling (if using)
scant 1⅝ cups all-purpose flour
1 tbsp baking powder
1 tbsp unsweetened cocoa

½ tsp allspice
2 large eggs
¾ cup unsweetened orange juice
1 tsp grated orange rind
⅝ cup fresh blueberries

Sugarless Chocolate Muffins

For a really deep chocolate experience, you can add a generous ½ cup sugar-free chocolate chips to this recipe. If you can't find sugar-free chocolate chips in your local stores, you can use a sugar-free chocolate bar instead. Simply cut off a piece of chocolate weighing 3½ oz/100 g, then chop it into smaller pieces. Gently stir them into the muffin batter just before dividing it between the paper liners, then bake in the usual way.

• Preheat the oven to 400°F/200°C. Oil a 12-cup muffin pan with sunflower-seed oil, or line it with 12 muffin paper liners. Sift the flour, baking powder, cocoa, and allspice into a large mixing bowl.

• In a separate bowl, whisk the eggs and the remaining sunflower-seed oil together. Pour in the orange juice, add the grated orange rind and the blueberries, and stir together gently to mix. Add the egg and fruit mixture to the flour mixture and then gently stir together until just combined. Do not overstir the batter—it is fine for it to be a little lumpy.

• Divide the muffin batter evenly between the 12 cups in the muffin pan or the paper liners (they should be about two-thirds full). Transfer to the oven and bake for 20 minutes, or until risen and golden. Remove the muffins from the oven and serve warm, or place them on a cooling rack and let cool.

MAKES 12

vegetable oil cooking spray,
   for oiling (if using)
1½ cups all-purpose flour
2 tsp baking powder
¼ tsp salt
½ tsp allspice

5 tbsp superfine sugar
2 large egg whites
2 ripe bananas, sliced
⅜ cup no-soak dried dates,
   pitted and chopped
4 tbsp skim milk
5 tbsp maple syrup

Lowfat Banana and Date Muffins

This recipe is excellent for people on a lowfat diet. It also works well without the dates. You can replace the dates with the same quantity of chopped dried figs or apricots.

• Preheat the oven to 400°F/200°C. Spray a 12-cup muffin pan with vegetable oil cooking spray, or line it with 12 muffin paper liners. Sift the flour, baking powder, salt, and allspice into a mixing bowl. Add the superfine sugar and mix together.

• In a separate bowl, whisk the egg whites together. Mash the sliced bananas in a separate bowl, then add them to the egg whites. Add the dates, then pour in the skim milk and maple syrup and stir together gently to mix. Add the banana and date mixture to the flour mixture and then gently stir together until just combined. Do not overstir the batter—it is fine for it to be a little lumpy.

• Divide the muffin batter evenly between the 12 cups in the muffin pan or the paper liners (they should be about two-thirds full). Transfer to the oven and bake for 25 minutes, or until risen and golden. Remove the muffins from the oven and serve warm, or place them on a cooling rack and let cool.

MAKES 12

vegetable oil cooking spray,
    for oiling (if using)

scant 1⅝ cups all-purpose flour

1 tsp baking soda

¼ tsp salt

1 tsp allspice

generous ½ cup superfine sugar

3 large egg whites

3 tbsp lowfat margarine

⅔ cup thick, lowfat, plain or
    blueberry-flavored yogurt

1 tsp vanilla extract

¾ cup fresh blueberries

Lowfat Blueberry Muffins

Another way to test that your muffins are cooked is to remove them from the oven at the end of the cooking time and insert a toothpick into the center of one of the muffins. If it comes out clean, the muffins are cooked. If it does not come out clean, then return the muffins to the oven and bake for a little longer.

• Preheat the oven to 375°F/190°C. Spray a 12-cup muffin pan with vegetable oil cooking spray, or line it with 12 muffin paper liners. Sift the flour, baking soda, salt, and half of the allspice into a large mixing bowl. Add 6 tablespoons of the superfine sugar and mix together.

• In a separate bowl, whisk the egg whites together. Add the margarine, yogurt, and vanilla extract and mix together well, then stir in the fresh blueberries until thoroughly mixed. Add the fruit mixture to the flour mixture and then gently stir together until just combined. Do not overstir the batter—it is fine for it to be a little lumpy.

• Divide the muffin batter evenly between the 12 cups in the muffin pan or the paper liners (they should be about two-thirds full). Mix the remaining sugar with the remaining allspice, then sprinkle the mixture over the muffins. Transfer to the oven and bake for 25 minutes, or until risen and golden. Remove the muffins from the oven and serve warm, or place them on a cooling rack and let cool.

MAKES 12

2 tbsp sunflower-seed or peanut oil,
   plus extra for oiling (if using)
scant ¾ cup all-purpose white flour
¾ cup all-purpose whole wheat flour
1 tsp baking soda
¼ tsp salt
1 tsp ground cinnamon
½ tsp ground ginger

2 tbsp superfine sugar
2 large egg whites
5 tbsp skim or lowfat milk
8 oz/225 g canned pineapple chunks
   in juice, drained and chopped
9 oz/250 g carrots, grated
¼ cup golden raisins
⅜ cup shelled walnuts, chopped

TOPPING

1⅛ cups Quark (or any lowfat
   soft cheese)
1½ tbsp superfine sugar
1½ tsp vanilla extract
1½ tsp ground cinnamon

Spiced Carrot Cake Muffins

If you are catering for a party, why not spoon the batter into mini-muffin pans instead? The batter will go a lot further and will create an abundance of mouthwatering morsels that will look good on any party buffet table.

• Preheat the oven to 375°F/190°C. Oil a 12-cup muffin pan with sunflower-seed oil, or line it with 12 muffin paper liners. Sift both flours, baking soda, salt, cinnamon, and ginger into a mixing bowl. Add the superfine sugar and mix together.

• In a separate bowl, whisk the egg whites together, then pour in the milk and remaining oil and mix together. Mash the pineapple chunks, then add to the egg mixture. Add the carrots, golden raisins, and walnuts and stir together gently. Add the fruit mixture to the flour mixture and then gently stir together until just combined. Do not overstir the batter—it is fine for it to be a little lumpy.

• Divide the muffin batter evenly between the 12 cups in the muffin pan or the paper liners (they should be about two-thirds full). Transfer to the oven and bake for 25 minutes, or until risen and golden.

• While the muffins are in the oven, make the topping. Place the Quark in a mixing bowl with the superfine sugar, vanilla extract, and 1 teaspoon of the cinnamon. Mix together well, then cover with plastic wrap and transfer to the refrigerator until ready to use.

• When the muffins are cooked, remove them from the oven, place them on a cooling rack, and let cool. When they have cooled to room temperature, remove the topping from the refrigerator and spread some evenly over the top of each muffin. Lightly sprinkle over the remaining cinnamon and serve.

MAKES 12

3 large baking apples, peeled
and cored

generous 1½ cups water

1½ tsp allspice

vegetable oil cooking spray,
for oiling (if using)

generous 2 cups all-purpose
whole wheat flour

1 tbsp baking powder

¼ tsp salt

3 tbsp superfine sugar

1⅛ cups fresh raspberries

Lowfat Apple and Raspberry Muffins

These delicious muffins are extremely low in fat and ideal for a lowfat diet. You can also vary the amount of sugar according to your taste. Try reducing the amount to 2 tablespoons for less sweetness, or increase it to 4 tablespoons for sweeter muffins.

• Thinly slice 2 baking apples and place them in a pan with 6 tablespoons of the water. Bring to a boil, then reduce the heat. Stir in ½ teaspoon of the allspice, cover the pan, and let simmer, stirring occasionally, for 15–20 minutes until the water has been absorbed. Remove from the heat and let cool. Transfer to a food processor and blend until smooth. Stir in the remaining water and mix well.

• Preheat the oven to 400°F/200°C. Spray a 12-cup muffin pan with vegetable oil cooking spray, or line it with 12 muffin paper liners. Sift the flour, baking powder, salt, and remaining allspice into a mixing bowl. Then stir in the sugar.

• Chop the remaining apple and add to the flour mixture. Add the raspberries, then combine gently with the flour mixture until lightly coated. Finally, gently stir in the cooled apple/water mixture. Do not overstir the batter—it is fine for it to be a little lumpy.

• Divide the muffin batter evenly between the 12 cups in the muffin pan or the paper liners (they should be about two-thirds full). Transfer to the oven and bake for 25 minutes, or until risen and golden. Remove the muffins from the oven and serve warm, or place them on a cooling rack and let cool.

For picnics and school lunch boxes, Saturday brunch for family and friends, or even an after-theater or post-movie evening snack, there are few things more appetizing and tempting than savory muffins. They're also the perfect choice, perhaps served with a steaming bowl of soup, on a cold winter's evening when you don't feel much like cooking and just want to snuggle on the sofa and watch your favorite television program.

Most people are familiar with the idea of cheese muffins—and there are some terrific recipes for these in this chapter—but the range of other flavors may well surprise you. Peckish meat-lovers are guaranteed to enjoy Spicy Chicken Muffins or Potato and Pancetta Muffins, while the vegetarian options include Italian Tomato Muffins or Sour Cream Muffins with Chives.

SAVORY MUFFINS

Savory muffins are also a great choice for breakfast, providing an energizing start to the day. More fun and more nourishing than cereals, they are also sure to be popular with all the family and are a good way to ring the changes without lots of extra effort. Everyone is certain to put their best foot forward when facing the day ahead if they've stoked up on freshly baked Bacon and Cornmeal Muffins or Herb Muffins with Smoked Cheese before leaving the house.

MAKES 10

generous ¾ cup self-rising flour

1 tbsp baking powder

1 tsp salt

1½ cups fine cornmeal

1⅜ cups grated sharp Cheddar
    cheese

4 tbsp butter, melted

2 large eggs, beaten

1 garlic clove, crushed

1¼ cups milk

Cheese Muffins

Cornmeal, or polenta, used to be difficult to find, but it is now widely available in most major supermarkets and health-food stores.

• Preheat the oven to 400°F/200°C. Line 10 cups of a 12-cup muffin pan with muffin paper liners. Sift the flour, baking powder, and salt into a bowl, then stir in the cornmeal and 1 cup of the cheese.

• Place the melted butter, eggs, crushed garlic, and milk in a separate bowl. Add the wet ingredients to the dry ingredients and mix gently until just combined.

• Divide the batter evenly between the paper liners, sprinkle over the remaining cheese, and bake in the oven for 20–25 minutes, or until risen and golden. Remove from the oven and serve warm, or place on a cooling rack and let cool.

MAKES 12

10½ oz/300 g Italian plum tomatoes

1 tbsp sunflower-seed or peanut oil,
for oiling (if using)

1 cup all-purpose flour

2 tbsp baking powder

½ tsp salt

scant 1⅓ cups fine cornmeal

1 large egg, lightly beaten

1¼ cups milk

1 garlic clove, crushed

1 tbsp chopped fresh basil

1½ tsp chopped fresh parsley

Italian Tomato Muffins

To peel tomatoes, bring a kettle of water to a boil. Place the tomatoes in a heatproof bowl, then pour over enough boiling water to cover them. Let them soak for about 3 minutes, then lift them out of the water and let cool slightly. When the tomatoes are cool enough to handle, gently pierce the skins with the tip of a knife. Remove and discard the skins.

• First peel the tomatoes (see note, left), then seed them (use a teaspoon for this). Chop the tomatoes finely and set aside.

• Preheat the oven to 400°F/200°C. Oil a 12-cup muffin pan with sunflower-seed oil, or line it with 12 muffin paper liners. Sift the flour, baking powder, and salt into a large mixing bowl. Then add the cornmeal and mix together well.

• In a separate bowl, lightly whisk the egg and the milk together with a fork. Add the reserved chopped tomatoes, then the garlic, basil, and parsley and mix together well. Add the egg and tomato mixture to the flour mixture and then gently stir together until just combined. Do not overstir the batter—it is fine for it to be a little lumpy.

• Divide the muffin batter evenly between the 12 cups in the muffin pan or the paper liners (they should be about two-thirds full). Transfer to the oven and bake for 20 minutes, or until risen and golden. Remove the muffins from the oven and serve warm, or place them on a cooling rack and let cool.

MAKES 12

1 tbsp sunflower-seed or peanut
   oil, for oiling (if using)
2 cups all-purpose flour
2 tsp baking powder
½ tsp baking soda
1 oz/25 g Cheddar cheese, grated

1¼ oz/35 g fresh chives, finely
   snipped, plus extra to garnish
1 large egg, lightly beaten
scant 1 cup sour cream
generous ⅓ cup plain unsweetened
   yogurt
4 tbsp butter, melted

Sour Cream Muffins with Chives

These muffins are deliciously creamy and a real treat for any picnic, buffet, or lunch box. For extra flavor, try stirring 2 tablespoons finely chopped scallion into the batter when you add the chives.

• Preheat the oven to 400°F/200°C. Oil a 12-cup muffin pan with sunflower-seed oil, or line it with 12 muffin paper liners. Sift the flour, baking powder, and baking soda into a large mixing bowl. Add the cheese and chives and mix together well.

• In a separate bowl, lightly mix the egg, sour cream, yogurt, and melted butter together. Add the sour cream mixture to the flour mixture and then gently stir together until just combined. Do not overstir the batter—it is fine for it to be a little lumpy.

• Divide the muffin batter evenly between the 12 cups in the muffin pan or the paper liners (they should be about two-thirds full). Sprinkle over the remaining snipped chives to garnish and transfer to the oven. Bake for 20 minutes, or until risen and golden. Remove the muffins from the oven and serve warm, or place them on a cooling rack and let cool.

MAKES 12

1 tbsp sunflower-seed or peanut
　oil, for oiling (if using)
2 cups all-purpose flour
2 tsp baking powder
½ tsp baking soda
1 oz/25 g smoked hard
　cheese, grated

1¾ oz/50 g fresh parsley, finely
　chopped
1 large egg, lightly beaten
1¼ cups thick strained plain yogurt
4 tbsp butter, melted

Herb Muffins with Smoked Cheese

The smoked cheese gives these muffins a wonderfully smoky flavor. If smoked cheese is unavailable, however, you can replace it with the same quantity of ordinary sharp Cheddar cheese.

• Preheat the oven to 400°F/200°C. Oil a 12-cup muffin pan with sunflower-seed oil, or line it with 12 muffin paper liners. Sift the flour, baking powder, and baking soda into a large mixing bowl. Add the smoked cheese and the parsley and mix together well.

• In a separate bowl, lightly mix the egg, yogurt, and melted butter together. Add the yogurt mixture to the flour mixture and then gently stir together until just combined. Do not overstir the batter—it is fine for it to be a little lumpy.

• Divide the muffin batter evenly between the 12 cups in the muffin pan or the paper liners (they should be about two-thirds full), then transfer to the oven. Bake for 20 minutes, or until risen and golden. Remove the muffins from the oven and serve warm, or place them on a cooling rack and let cool.

MAKES 12

2/3 cup sunflower-seed or peanut oil,
    plus extra for oiling (if using)

2 cups all-purpose flour

1 tbsp baking powder

½ tsp salt

3 tbsp granulated sugar

2 large eggs

¾ cup milk

14 oz/400 g zucchini, coarsely grated

1 oz/25 g manchego cheese, grated

2 tbsp chopped fresh flat-leaf parsley

Spanish Manchego Muffins

To ring the changes, try varying the flavor by replacing the chopped parsley with the same quantity of other chopped fresh herbs, such as oregano, rosemary, or basil.

• Preheat the oven to 400°F/200°C. Oil a 12-cup muffin pan with sunflower-seed oil, or line it with 12 muffin paper liners. Sift the flour, baking powder, and salt into a large mixing bowl. Add the sugar and mix together well.

• In a separate bowl, lightly beat the eggs. Stir in the milk and remaining sunflower-seed oil and mix together. Add the egg mixture to the flour mixture and then gently stir together. Gently stir in the zucchini, manchego cheese, and chopped parsley until just combined. Do not overstir the batter—it is fine for it to be a little lumpy.

• Divide the muffin batter evenly between the 12 cups in the muffin pan or the paper liners (they should be about two-thirds full), then transfer to the oven. Bake for 25 minutes, or until risen and golden. Remove the muffins from the oven and serve warm, or place them on a cooling rack and let cool.

MAKES 12

1 tbsp sunflower-seed or peanut oil,
    for oiling (if using)

2 cups all-purpose flour

1½ tsp baking powder

½ tsp baking soda

½ tsp salt

1 large egg

⅔ cup plain yogurt

⅔ cup sour cream

1 oz/25 g Cheddar cheese, grated

⅜ cup chopped fresh parsley

⅜ cup chopped fresh dill

CRAB AND CREAM
CHEESE FILLING

7 oz/200 g canned crabmeat, drained

⅞ cup cream cheese

2 tbsp mayonnaise

salt and pepper

Crab and Cream Cheese Muffins

For a salmon filling, replace the canned crabmeat with the same quantity of canned salmon, and stir in 1 tablespoon chopped fresh dill. For a tuna filling, replace the crabmeat with the same quantity of canned tuna, and stir in 4 tablespoons canned corn.

• Preheat the oven to 400°F/200°C. Oil a 12-cup muffin pan with sunflower-seed oil, or line it with 12 muffin paper liners. Sift the flour, baking powder, baking soda, and salt into a large mixing bowl.

• In a separate bowl, lightly beat the egg, then pour in the yogurt and sour cream and mix together. Stir in the grated cheese and chopped herbs. Add the sour cream and cheese mixture to the flour mixture, then gently stir together. Do not overstir the batter—it is fine for it to be a little lumpy.

• Divide the muffin batter evenly between the 12 cups in the muffin pan or the paper liners (they should be about two-thirds full), then transfer to the oven. Bake for 20 minutes, or until risen and golden.

• While the muffins are cooking, make the crab and cream cheese filling. Place the crabmeat in a mixing bowl and flake with a fork. Add the cream cheese and mayonnaise and mix together well. Season to taste with salt and pepper. Cover the bowl with plastic wrap and let chill in the refrigerator until ready for use.

• When the muffins are cooked, remove them from the oven, place them on a cooling rack, and let cool to room temperature. When they have cooled, cut them in half horizontally. Remove the crabmeat filling from the refrigerator and spread it over the bottom halves of the muffins. Replace the top halves, so that the filling is sandwiched in the middle, and serve.

MAKES 12

½ cup sunflower-seed or peanut oil,
    plus extra for oiling

2 onions, chopped

3 scallions, chopped

1 small fresh red chili, seeded and
    finely chopped

3 skinless, boneless chicken thighs,
    chopped into small pieces

1 tsp paprika

scant 2¼ cups self-rising flour

1 tsp baking powder

2 large eggs

1 tbsp lemon juice

1 tbsp grated lemon rind

½ cup sour cream

½ cup plain yogurt

salt and pepper

Spicy Chicken Muffins

These muffins can be served warm, but they are also good served cold in lunch boxes and on picnics. If you haven't got a fresh red chili, simply omit it and replace the paprika with 1 teaspoon mild chili powder.

• Preheat the oven to 375°F/190°C. Oil a 12-cup muffin pan with sunflower-seed oil. Heat a little of the remaining oil in a skillet, add the onions, scallions, and chili, and cook over low heat, stirring constantly, for 3 minutes.

• Remove from the heat, lift out the onions and chili, and set aside. Heat a little more of the remaining oil in the skillet, add the chicken and paprika, and cook, stirring, over medium heat for 5 minutes. Remove from the heat and set aside.

• Sift the flour and baking powder into a large mixing bowl. In a separate bowl, lightly beat the eggs, then stir in the remaining oil and the lemon juice and rind. Pour in the sour cream and the yogurt and mix together. Add the egg mixture to the flour mixture, then gently stir in the onions, scallions, chili, and chicken. Season to taste with salt and pepper. Do not overstir the batter—it is fine for it to be a little lumpy.

• Divide the muffin batter evenly between the 12 cups in the muffin pan (they should reach the top), then transfer to the oven. Bake for 20 minutes, or until risen and golden. Remove the muffins from the oven and serve warm, or place them on a cooling rack and let cool.

MAKES 12

2 tbsp sunflower-seed or peanut oil, plus extra for oiling (if using)

1 leek, washed, trimmed, and finely chopped

2 cups all-purpose flour

2 tsp baking powder

½ tsp baking soda

1 large egg, lightly beaten

1¼ cups thick strained plain yogurt

4 tbsp butter, melted

1 oz/25 g Cheddar cheese, grated

1 oz/25 g fresh chives, finely snipped

5½ oz/150 g cooked ham, chopped

Savory Leek and Ham Muffins

Cooked bacon works as well as ham in these muffins. You can also replace some or all of the Cheddar cheese with a smoked cheese for an added smoky flavor.

• Preheat the oven to 400°F/200°C. Oil a 12-cup muffin pan with sunflower-seed oil, or line it with 12 muffin paper liners. Heat the remaining oil in a skillet, add the chopped leek, and cook, stirring, over low heat for 2 minutes. Remove from the heat and let cool.

• Sift the flour, baking powder, and baking soda into a large mixing bowl. In a separate bowl, lightly mix the egg, yogurt, and melted butter together. Add the Cheddar cheese, chives, cooked leek, and half of the chopped ham, then mix together well. Add the cheese mixture to the flour mixture and then gently stir together until just combined. Do not overstir the batter—it is fine for it to be a little lumpy.

• Divide the muffin batter evenly between the 12 cups in the muffin pan or the paper liners (they should be about two-thirds full). Sprinkle over the remaining chopped ham, then transfer to the oven. Bake for 20 minutes, or until risen and golden. Remove the muffins from the oven and serve warm, or place them on a cooling rack and let cool.

MAKES 12

5½ oz/150 g pancetta

generous 1 cup self-rising flour

1 tbsp baking powder

1 tsp salt

generous 1⅔ cups fine cornmeal

generous ¼ cup golden granulated
  sugar

3½ oz/100 g butter, melted

2 large eggs, beaten

1¼ cups milk

Bacon and Cornmeal Muffins

Pancetta is thin Italian bacon. If it is unavailable, you can use thinly sliced pieces of lean bacon instead.

• Preheat the oven to 400°F/200°C and preheat the broiler to medium. Line a 12-cup muffin pan with muffin paper liners. Cook the pancetta under the preheated broiler until crisp and then crumble into pieces. Set aside until required.

• Sift the flour, baking powder, and salt into a bowl, then stir in the cornmeal and sugar. Place the butter, eggs, and milk in a separate bowl. Add the wet ingredients to the dry ingredients and mix until just blended.

• Fold in the crumbled pancetta, then divide the muffin batter between the paper liners and bake in the oven for 20–25 minutes until risen and golden. Remove the muffins from the oven and serve warm, or place them on a cooling rack and let cool.

MAKES 12

1 tbsp sunflower-seed or peanut oil,
plus extra for oiling (if using)

3 shallots, finely chopped

2⅜ cups self-rising flour

1 tsp salt

1 lb/450 g potatoes, cooked
and mashed

2 large eggs

1½ cups milk

½ cup sour cream

1 tbsp finely snipped fresh chives

5½ oz/150 g pancetta, broiled and
crumbled into pieces

4 tbsp grated Cheddar cheese

Potato and Pancetta Muffins

To make a lower-fat version of these muffins, use muffin paper liners and cook the shallots in vegetable oil cooking spray instead of sunflower-seed oil. Use lowfat or skim milk instead of whole milk, and replace the sour cream with the same quantity of thick strained plain yogurt. Finally, use a lowfat Cheddar cheese, or omit the cheese altogether.

• Preheat the oven to 400°F/200°C. Oil a 12-cup muffin pan with sunflower-seed oil, or line it with 12 muffin paper liners. Heat the remaining oil in a skillet, add the chopped shallots, and cook, stirring, over low heat for 2 minutes. Remove from the heat and let cool.

• Sift the flour and salt into a large mixing bowl. In a separate bowl, mix the mashed potatoes, eggs, milk, sour cream, chives, and half of the pancetta together. Add the potato mixture to the flour mixture and then gently stir together until just combined. Do not overstir the batter—it is fine for it to be a little lumpy.

• Divide the muffin batter evenly between the 12 cups in the muffin pan or the paper liners (they should be about two-thirds full). Sprinkle over the remaining pancetta, then sprinkle over the grated Cheddar cheese. Transfer to the oven and bake for 20 minutes, or until risen and golden. Remove the muffins from the oven and serve warm, or place them on a cooling rack and let cool.

A celebration tea party, a fund-raising coffee morning, a Mother's Day breakfast in bed, stocking the cake stall at the school

summer fair—these are just some of the reasons why you might want to push the boat out with this mouthwatering collection of

extra-special muffins. In fact, baking a batch of these superb tempting treats will turn any occasion into a special one. If you can

bear to part with them, you could even pack them into a pretty box to make a charming gift.

Some of these recipes are strictly for adults only. Rice Muffins with Amaretto, for example, are served with a luxurious

almond-flavored liqueur butter, and the recipe titles Irish Coffee Muffins and Apricot Muffins with Cointreau speak for

themselves. The wickedly indulgent Triple Chocolate Muffins, on the other hand, will appeal to chocoholics of any age.

SPECIAL OCCASIONS

Sweetly scented cakes flavored with edible flowers, such as the delightfully dainty Frosted Lavender Muffins, make a stylish

addition to the tea table redolent of a more gracious age of silver services, porcelain cups, crisp linen, and rolling country house

lawns, while Mocha Muffins are just designed for a cosy, gossipy coffee morning with the neighbors. But, in fact, you don't need

an excuse to enjoy these fabulous confections—simply making them in the first place is celebration enough.

MAKES 9

butter, for greasing

1 cup all-purpose flour

1 tbsp baking powder

½ tsp baking soda

½ tsp salt

1 large egg

4 tbsp honey

½ cup milk

2 tbsp sunflower-seed or peanut oil

½ tsp almond extract

¾ cup cooked risotto rice

2–3 amaretti cookies, coarsely
    crushed

AMARETTO BUTTER

1 tbsp honey

1–2 tbsp amaretto

½ cup mascarpone cheese

Rice Muffins with Amaretto

Italian rice gives these delicate muffins an interesting texture. The amaretti cookies complement their flavor and add a crunchy topping.

• Preheat the oven to 400°F/200°C. Grease 9 cups of a 12-cup muffin pan with butter. Sift the flour, baking powder, baking soda, and salt into a large bowl and stir. Make a well in the center.

• In a separate bowl, beat the egg, honey, milk, oil, and almond extract with an electric whisk for about 2 minutes, or until light and foamy. Gradually beat in the rice. Pour into the well in the dry ingredients and, using a fork, stir lightly until just combined. Do not beat too long or the batter can become lumpy.

• Divide the batter evenly between the 9 cups in the muffin pan. Sprinkle each with some of the amaretti crumbs and bake for 15 minutes until risen and golden. The tops should spring back when pressed. Remove from the oven and cool in the pan for about 1 minute. Carefully remove the muffins and let cool slightly.

• To make the Amaretto butter, place the honey, amaretto, and mascarpone in a small bowl and beat together. Spoon into a small serving bowl and serve with the warm muffins.

MAKES 12

generous 1¾ cups all-purpose flour

⅓ cup unsweetened cocoa

2 tsp baking powder

½ tsp baking soda

generous ½ cup semisweet
    chocolate chips

generous ½ cup white
    chocolate chips

2 large eggs, beaten

1¼ cups sour cream

generous ⅜ cup packed brown sugar

3 oz/85 g butter, melted

Triple Chocolate Muffins

Packed with melting semisweet and white chocolate, these creamy muffins are a chocoholic's delight. Serve with coffee for a real treat.

• Preheat the oven to 400°F/200°C. Line a 12-cup muffin pan with muffin paper liners. Sift the flour, cocoa, baking powder, and baking soda into a large bowl, add the semisweet and white chocolate chips, and stir.

• Place the eggs, sour cream, sugar, and melted butter in a separate mixing bowl and mix well. Add the wet ingredients to the dry ingredients and stir gently until just combined.

• Using 2 spoons, divide the batter evenly between the paper liners and bake in the preheated oven for 20 minutes, or until well risen and firm to the touch. Remove from the oven and serve warm, or place on a cooling rack and let cool.

MAKES 12

2½ oz/70 g butter

2 cups all-purpose flour

6 tbsp unsweetened cocoa

3 tsp baking powder

generous ⅜ cup superfine sugar

generous ½ cup milk chocolate chips

¼ cup multicolored mini
    marshmallows

1 large egg, beaten

1¼ cups milk

Marshmallow Muffins

Don't overbeat the batter
(there should still be a few
lumps of flour) or the
muffins will be crusty.

• Preheat the oven to 375°F/190°C. Line a 12-cup muffin pan with muffin paper liners. Melt the butter in a pan.

• Sift the flour, cocoa, and baking powder together into a large bowl. Stir in the sugar, chocolate chips, and marshmallows until thoroughly mixed.

• Whisk the egg, milk, and melted butter together in a separate bowl, then gently stir into the flour to form a stiff batter. Divide the batter evenly between the muffin liners.

• Bake in the oven for 20–25 minutes until well risen and golden brown. Remove from the oven and let cool in the pan for 5 minutes, then place on a cooling rack and let cool completely.

MAKES 12

1 tbsp sunflower-seed or peanut oil,
   for oiling (if using)
generous 1¾ cups all-purpose flour
1 tsp baking powder
1 tsp baking soda
½ tsp allspice
4 oz/115 g butter
1 cup packed brown sugar

2 large eggs, beaten
2 tbsp thick plain, banana, or
   pineapple-flavored yogurt
1 tbsp rum
1 ripe banana, sliced
2¾ oz/75 g canned pineapple rings,
   drained and chopped
⅜ cup dry unsweetened coconut

COCONUT TOPPING
4 tbsp raw sugar
1 tsp allspice
scant ¼ cup dry unsweetened
   coconut

Tropical Coconut Muffins

To make these muffins without the alcohol, perhaps for a children's party, replace the rum with 1 teaspoon almond extract and 2 teaspoons milk.

• Preheat the oven to 400°F/200°C. Oil a 12-cup muffin pan with sunflower-seed oil, or line it with 12 muffin paper liners. Sift the flour, baking powder, baking soda, and allspice into a mixing bowl.

• In a separate large bowl, cream together the butter and brown sugar, then stir in the eggs, yogurt, and rum. Add the banana, pineapple, and dry unsweetened coconut and mix together gently. Add the pineapple mixture to the flour mixture and then gently stir together until just combined. Do not overstir the batter—it is fine for it to be a little lumpy.

• Divide the muffin batter evenly between the 12 cups in the muffin pan or the paper liners (they should be about two-thirds full). To make the topping, mix the raw sugar and allspice together and sprinkle over the muffins. Sprinkle over the dry unsweetened coconut, then transfer to the preheated oven. Bake for 20 minutes, or until risen and golden. Remove the muffins from the oven and serve warm, or place them on a cooling rack and let cool.

MAKES 12

1 large baking apple, peeled, cored,
    and thinly sliced

3 tbsp water

1 tbsp sunflower-seed or peanut oil,
    for oiling (if using)

1 cup all-purpose flour

1 tsp baking powder

1 tsp baking soda

pinch of salt

4 tbsp butter

4 tbsp superfine sugar

1 large egg, beaten

½ tsp vanilla extract

1 tbsp dried lavender flowers

LAVENDER FROSTING

⅞ cup confectioners' sugar

1 tbsp dried lavender flowers

1 tbsp liquid glucose

1–2 tbsp milk

Frosted Lavender Muffins

To give a deeper color to these muffins, pour a few drops of liquid lavender food coloring into the frosting along with the milk, then stir together well.

• The day before you need to make these muffins, start preparing the frosting. Place the confectioners' sugar in a bowl, then add the dried lavender flowers. Cover with plastic wrap and leave overnight until ready for use.

• When you are ready to make the muffins, place the sliced baking apple and water in a pan and bring to a boil. Reduce the heat, cover the pan, and let simmer for 15–20 minutes, stirring occasionally, until the water has been absorbed. Remove from the heat and let cool. Transfer to a food processor and process until smooth.

• Preheat the oven to 400°F/200°C. Oil a 12-cup muffin pan with sunflower-seed oil, or line it with 12 muffin paper liners. Sift the flour, baking powder, baking soda, and salt into a mixing bowl.

• In a separate large bowl, cream together the butter and superfine sugar, then stir in the beaten egg, vanilla extract, apple purée, and dried lavender flowers, stripped from their stalks. Add the egg mixture to the flour mixture and then gently stir together until just combined. Do not overstir the batter—it is fine for it to be a little lumpy.

• Divide the muffin batter evenly between the 12 cups in the muffin pan or the paper liners (they should be about two-thirds full). Transfer to the oven and bake for 20 minutes, or until risen and golden.

• While the muffins are cooking, finish making the frosting. Remove the plastic wrap from the confectioners' sugar/lavender mixture, then sift the mixture into a bowl and discard the lavender flowers. Stir in the liquid glucose and enough milk to make the frosting easy to spread. Cover with plastic wrap until ready to use.

• When the muffins are cooked, remove them from the oven, place them on a cooling rack, and let cool. When they have cooled completely, spread each muffin with some of the lavender frosting and serve.

MAKES 12

1 tbsp sunflower-seed or peanut oil,
   for oiling (if using)

1½ cups all-purpose flour

2 tsp baking powder

pinch of salt

4 tbsp butter

6 tbsp superfine sugar

1 large egg, beaten

½ cup milk

1 tsp rose water

1¾ oz/50 g edible rose petals, rinsed,
   patted dry, and lightly snipped

ROSE PETAL FROSTING

⅞ cup confectioners' sugar

1 tbsp liquid glucose

1 tbsp rose water

1¾ oz/50 g edible rose petals,
   rinsed and patted dry

Rose Petal Muffins

You can also make one spectacular large muffin with these ingredients. Place the muffin batter in an oiled 9-inch/23-cm pie dish, then bake in the usual way.

• Preheat the oven to 400°F/200°C. Oil a 12-cup muffin pan with sunflower-seed oil, or line it with 12 muffin paper liners. Sift the flour, baking powder, and salt into a large mixing bowl.

• In a separate large bowl, cream together the butter and superfine sugar, then stir in the beaten egg, milk, rose water, and snipped rose petals. Add the butter mixture to the flour mixture and then gently stir together until just combined. Do not overstir the batter—it is fine for it to be a little lumpy.

• Divide the muffin batter evenly between the 12 cups in the muffin pan or the paper liners (they should be about two-thirds full). Transfer to the oven and bake for 20 minutes, or until risen and golden.

• While the muffins are cooking, make the frosting. Place the confectioners' sugar in a bowl, then stir in the liquid glucose and rose water. Cover with plastic wrap until ready to use.

• When the muffins are cooked, remove them from the oven, place on a cooling rack, and let cool. When they have cooled, spread each muffin with some of the frosting, strew over and/or around with the rose petals, and serve.

MAKES 12

1 tbsp sunflower-seed or peanut oil, for oiling (if using)

2 cups all-purpose flour

1 tbsp baking powder

pinch of salt

3 oz/85 g butter

generous ⅜ cup raw sugar

1 large egg, beaten

½ cup heavy cream

1 tsp almond extract

2 tbsp strong coffee

2 tbsp coffee-flavored liqueur

4 tbsp Irish whiskey or similar whiskey

Irish Coffee Muffins

To make these muffins even more luxurious, let them cool, then slice them in half horizontally and fill them with freshly whipped cream (sweetened with a little sugar if necessary).

For a lower-fat muffin, leave out the filling and replace the heavy cream with the same quantity of lower-fat light cream.

• Preheat the oven to 400°F/200°C. Oil a 12-cup muffin pan with sunflower-seed oil, or line it with 12 muffin paper liners. Sift the flour, baking powder, and salt into a large mixing bowl.

• In a separate large bowl, cream the butter and raw sugar together, then stir in the beaten egg. Pour in the heavy cream, almond extract, coffee, liqueur, and whiskey and stir together. Add the whiskey mixture to the flour mixture and then gently stir together until just combined. Do not overstir the batter—it is fine for it to be a little lumpy.

• Divide the muffin batter evenly between the 12 cups in the muffin pan or the paper liners (they should be about two-thirds full). Transfer to the oven and bake for 20 minutes, or until risen and golden. Remove the muffins from the oven and serve warm, or place them on a cooling rack and let cool.

MAKES 12

1 tbsp sunflower-seed or peanut
   oil, for oiling (if using)
scant 1 cup self-rising flour
2 tsp baking powder
6 oz/175 g butter
scant ⅔ cup superfine sugar
2 large eggs, beaten

½ cup milk
4 tbsp light cream
1 tbsp orange-flavored liqueur,
   such as Cointreau
generous ½ cup no-soak dried
   apricots, chopped
generous ½ cup no-soak dried
   dates, pitted and chopped

CINNAMON TOPPING

3 tbsp raw sugar
1 tsp ground cinnamon
1 tbsp freshly grated orange rind

Apricot Muffins with Cointreau

If you would prefer to make these muffins without the alcohol, replace the orange-flavored liqueur with 1 tablespoon fresh unsweetened orange juice and 1 tablespoon grated orange rind.

• Preheat the oven to 375°F/190°C. Oil a 12-cup muffin pan with sunflower-seed oil, or line it with 12 muffin paper liners. Sift the flour and baking powder into a large mixing bowl.

• In a separate large bowl, cream together the butter and superfine sugar, then stir in the beaten eggs. Pour in the milk, cream, and orange-flavored liqueur, then add the chopped apricots and dates and gently mix together. Add the fruit mixture to the flour mixture and then gently stir together until just combined. Do not overstir the batter—it is fine for it to be a little lumpy.

• Divide the muffin batter evenly between the 12 cups in the muffin pan or the paper liners (they should be about two-thirds full). To make the topping, place the raw sugar in a small bowl, then mix in the cinnamon and orange rind. Sprinkle the topping over the muffins, then transfer to the oven and bake for 20 minutes, or until risen and golden. Remove the muffins from the oven and serve warm, or place them on a cooling rack and let cool.

MAKES 12

1 tbsp sunflower-seed or peanut oil,
    for oiling (if using)

scant 1⅝ cups all-purpose flour

1 tbsp baking powder

pinch of salt

3 tbsp butter

2 tbsp superfine sugar

1 large egg, beaten

scant 1 cup milk

2 tsp cherry brandy

10½ oz/300 g drained canned
    cherries, chopped

Brandied Cherry Muffins

These muffins are delicious served with freshly whipped cream or spoonfuls of fresh mascarpone cheese. Serve the cream or mascarpone alongside the muffins or, for extra decorative flair, let the muffins cool, halve them horizontally, then spread the cream or mascarpone over the cut sides of the bases. Top with the other muffin halves, and serve.

• Preheat the oven to 400°F/200°C. Oil a 12-cup muffin pan with sunflower-seed oil, or line it with 12 muffin paper liners. Sift the flour, baking powder, and salt into a large mixing bowl.

• In a separate large bowl, cream the butter and superfine sugar together, then stir in the beaten egg. Pour in the milk and cherry brandy, then add the chopped cherries and gently stir together. Add the cherry mixture to the flour mixture and then gently stir together until just combined. Do not overstir the batter—it is fine for it to be a little lumpy.

• Divide the muffin batter evenly between the 12 cups in the muffin pan or the paper liners (they should be about two-thirds full). Transfer to the oven and bake for 20–25 minutes until risen and golden. Remove the muffins from the oven and serve warm, or place them on a cooling rack and let cool.

MAKES 12

1 tbsp sunflower-seed or peanut oil,
　for oiling (if using)

generous 1¾ cups all-purpose flour

1 tbsp baking powder

2 tbsp unsweetened cocoa

pinch of salt

4 oz/115 g butter, melted

scant ¾ cup raw sugar

1 large egg, beaten

1 cup milk

1 tsp almond extract

2 tbsp strong coffee

1 tbsp instant coffee powder

generous ¼ cup semisweet
　chocolate chips

scant ⅓ cup raisins

COCOA TOPPING

3 tbsp raw sugar

1 tbsp unsweetened cocoa

1 tsp allspice

Mocha Muffins

To increase the protein content of these muffins and change the flavor and texture, replace the raisins with the same quantity of chopped almonds or walnuts, or use half raisins and half almonds/walnuts.

• Preheat the oven to 375°F/190°C. Oil a 12-cup muffin pan with sunflower-seed oil, or line it with 12 muffin paper liners. Sift the flour, baking powder, cocoa, and salt into a large mixing bowl.

• In a separate large bowl, cream the butter and raw sugar together, then stir in the beaten egg. Pour in the milk, almond extract, and coffee, then add the coffee powder, chocolate chips, and raisins and gently mix together. Add the raisin mixture to the flour mixture and then gently stir together until just combined. Do not overstir the batter—it is fine for it to be a little lumpy.

• Divide the muffin batter evenly between the 12 cups in the muffin pan or the paper liners (they should be about two-thirds full). To make the topping, place the raw sugar in a bowl, add the cocoa and allspice, and mix together well. Sprinkle the topping over the muffins, then transfer to the oven and bake for 20 minutes, or until risen and golden. Remove the muffins from the oven and serve warm, or place them on a cooling rack and let cool.

Index